A tree for thought

Alison Bonasoro

BookLeaf
Publishing

Presentation by *BookLeaf Publishing*

Web: www.bookleafpub.com

E-mail: info@bookleafpub.com

ISBN: 9789358735611

First edition 2023

I would like this book to be dedicated to anyone on a journey of self-discovery.

ACKNOWLEDGEMENT

Writing these pieces took a lot of thought and heart and honestly tears. It was a wonderful process and as much as they mirror each other they are all unique like each path in a forest is unique.

PREFACE

With these poems I hope someone who reads them can relate to what it feels like to not have it all figured out. As well as realizing that it's okay to still be searching and figuring it all out. Life is a journey of twists and turns and all things dark and beautiful.

Where I've been

I'm not gonna lie
I've been in the forest of knowing
Trees were bare and paths unclear
I fell down the whole of past time
Wandering the caves of hope
I'm not gonna lie
Maybe there's a glimpse of sight
Maybe it will come to me one night

I'm not gonna lie
After all the time in the forest
What I was hoping to know is still unknown
I'm not gonna lie if you ask about it
I'm not gonna lie,
I know I've squandered time

More than me

I don't want to be a cloudy day
I don't want to be the foolish sun-
The one that shines just to set
I want to be more than the storm you hate to
love and love to hate
To be the effects they give you
Not the havoc they cause
To live as vibrant as the awoken hues because
the sun chose to shine against the charcoal sky
I need to be as valuable as rain and as
appreciated as the sun
Because for once half is worse than nothing or
not at all

Dreaming of being

They say it's beautiful
I say it can be
To always be the dreamer
To be able to be in the darkest of hours
And see stars in the fragments of the breaking
Being the dreamer and turning the demons into
creatures of wisdom and guidance because there
has to be hope
To be the dreamer and feel the summer sun
instead of the heat of rage when you can't
escape

I get to be the dreamer
I can dream and dream and dream again
I can dream and hope one day my reality will be
better than what's in my head
They say it's beautiful

To be the dreamer
I say it can't be
Sometimes the dreamer wants to be the dream

Human nature

It's an Earthquake
It's a storm rolling in
It's a normal sunny day
And a break into gentle rain
It's a landslide then a hurricane
And all I can do is float on the waves

Faith, trust and no dust

What happens when a fairy doesn't get their full
wings?
They are limited to where they can go; to what
they can be.
Do they worry if they will?
Do they know why they didn't?
Do they fear being forgotten?
Are they as mythical as they feel?
They say everything changes once a Fairy gets
their full wings.
They are no longer stuck in the world they
always knew.
It's scary and exciting and they finally feel free
to be whomever they wish to be.
Gardeners, protectors, fighters; teachers;
anything is possible.
A limited one however;
Protects themselves,

Fights for themselves,
Inspires others to hope they get theirs because
they fear one day they'll be left and forgotten.
A fairy knows the day will come when they need
to say goodbye
They just never anticipate the forever.

Vines of the heart

She stands strong,
And weeps with the Willows.
For she knows as long as
He keeps her canopy intact
She could never shelter another

Color blind

It used to be so colorful
The way the world was
A purple tree
Blue skies and Monarch Butterflies
All the markers bleed
They bleed but not once did they blend
I could see every color
I could see it all
The purple tree,
Oh how real to a girl who lives to color

Only grey skies and not so many Butterflies
Is it markers or a marker?
can't see the hues
am I finally colorblind

Levels of being

It's a slow dance
It's the calming melodies on a Sunday
A gentle stand still on a rainy afternoon
The sand being pulled from under feet on the
shore
A baby grip on your finger
The warm summer breeze at night
All the little easy moments we take for granted

It's the class at 12
The learning at 14
The merging at 18
To the rush hour at 25
Only to be stuck in traffic for who knows how
long
Hoping for billboards along the way to show
something helpful
There's some hope
Take the exit- maybe better luck next time

Over and over again
Where are the exits to these little easy moments?

Still climbing

Hey there old friend.
How are you?

Oh me, ya know it comes and goes.

Ya, I remember the tree we used to climb, well
tried to climb.

You know we were never good at that.
We'd get to the first, maybe the second branch if
we were lucky.

Haha. Ya, it definitely felt like we were on top of
the world.

No, I don't know why I couldn't climb higher.
Do you?

Maybe I could now if I tried.

I know, the view must have been crazy up there.

Maybe things would be different if we tried
then.

Ya, I must have just been scared and felt like I
did my best.
You know me, always did the bare minimum to
get by haha.

Climbed those branches just to say I did.
That seems to be the one constant in us.

Ya, I'll try to climb higher.

First to forgive

She always apologized when she shouldn't
forgave.
She always forgave when there was no apology.
She accepts other's mistakes
Because she is made to feel like a machine; Easy
to overuse and ought to be perfect.
When she starts to break she knows what it's
like to feel worthless.
So for her everything is priceless.
Confrontation is a skill she never honed
But maybe it's time for her to walk alone.
She knows there's nothing left to say
She knows "I'm sorry" isn't enough
She knows there is nothing left.
Nothing to apologize for,
Nothing to forgive.
She just hopes that when she stops
She won't just be thrown away.

Articulate intention

Stop crying or stop trying?
They both sound the same
"Get out of your head"
Guess I'm the only one to blame.
You ask if I'm on meds
Because I can't keep holding it all in.
Yes, I'm always frustrated and overwhelmed
And I can't articulate why;
Or, maybe I can.
And it's within your comprehension that lies the
most tension.

One more chance

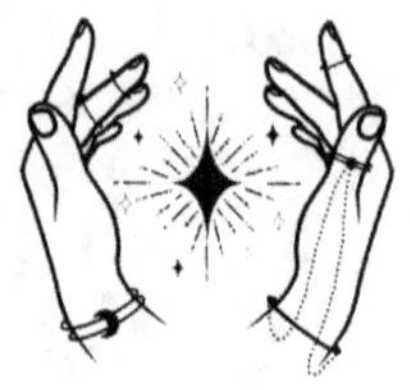

If you give me the stars
You won't see anymore scars.
I don't need to be kept blank,
I'm not an animal meant to be confined to a
tank.
Yes I struggle climbing these hills.
But I don't feel like myself when I'm stuck on
these pills.
I know they mean no harm,
And what happened isn't fair to my arm.
But If you give me the stars
I promise I'll shine.
All you have to do is look at the night sky.

Lost innocence

And she used to believe;
In magic
In the universe
In Heaven
But never Hell.
She believed that life,
As pure and warm as the Sun.
All the good in the beauty of the world could
never be damned.

Cold burn

The cold sets in deeper
I shrink into myself
Small enough to get lost in blankets
The cold sets in deeper
No amount of blankets can ease
It's not the change in weather that freezes me out
It's not that we succumb to the cold and early
darkness
It's not that seasonal
Sixteen months and fifteen days
It all adds up; every dig, every scrape and knock
Every memory - long and short
Deeper and deeper into the cold
The only relief is the warmth of the flame

Magic of familiarity

It's hard to find magic as you get older
I swear I found it long ago
Believing in the ending
So I kept that path in the back of my mind
Branching out on other trails
But always circled back to the one I knew I
belonged on
Some call that self sabotaging the possibility of
a better destination
But I kept telling myself I will end up on that
path no matter how long it took
One afternoon
I saw that path out of the corner of my eye
Did everything I could to get there
But it's a bumpy road and I feel like I'm
stumbling over rocks and roots
Getting stuck in a pothole of a fantasy I dug way
back when
Maybe that's all it was; Maybe that's what it's
suppose to be; A fantasy, a dream, not reality

A moment of solitude

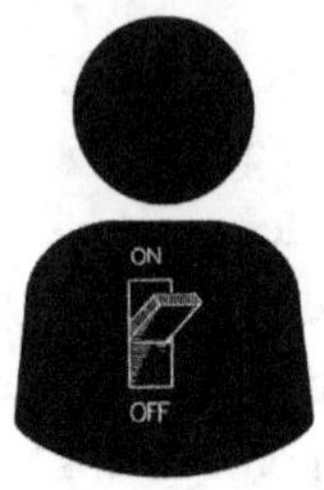

If I could just turn it off, just once.
Just for a little while.
Are you surprised I wouldn't have to think about
it.
Just for a chance to be anywhere else.
Just for a moment to feel something.
I would take that escape over anything.
Just for a moment.

One Day

One day I'll stop,
Stop hoping for things to change.
Stop wishing that everything will feel okay.
One day I'll accept,
Accept that everything changed and nothing is
going back to how it was.
Accept that nothing will feel okay because of it.
I'll accept it because I know everything always
feels off after any change and
You just adapt and feel what's now becoming
constant.

Filling

It was never supposed to be forever.
It was just a temporary fix.
I fell into the familiar comfort.
The routine I was craving.
But this craving turned into a cavity in my life,
And I don't know how to fix it.

I accept

If I gave you my reasons
You'd say they're excuses.
Fine I accept.
I accept the realism of your reality
Like I wish you would mine.
I accept your reaction
Like I wish you would mine.
I accept that you don't understand my choice
Because I didn't yours; for the longest time.
But I hope one day you will accept this for what
it was and not what you make it out to be.

Dream of light

I'll sit in the silence and eavesdrop on their
whispers.
I'll lay in the dark and pretend that it's over.
And in my dreams I'll succumb to this fight.
I'm not giving up or giving in.
For once I'm hoping that I'll wake up.

Trying to navigate

You ask if I'm even trying
And I say yes.
You ask again and I say yes.
You ask again and again and again.
As if you expect me to say something different.
I've always been alone here.
A solo journey I never had to question how to
navigate.
But I'm trying.
Trying not to trip over these roots.
Trying to find shelter before the dark
And trying to find something more comforting
than tree bark.
So forgive me for not trying at the same things
you are.